SCOTS PROVERBS
and Rhymes

BY THE SAME AUTHOR

Scots Proverbs and Rhymes	Moray Press (1948)
	W & R Chambers (1962)
	W & R Chambers (1970)
	The Pinetree Press (1976)
	Gordon Wright Publishing (1979)
	Gordon Wright Publishing (1983)
Doric Spice	Blackford Press (1956)
	The Pinetree Press (1960)
The Gowks of Moudieknowes	The Pinetree Press (1963)
What is Education in Scotland	Akros Publications (1970)
Macgregor's Mixture	Gordon Wright Publishing (1976)
Clan Gregor	The Clan Gregor Society (1977)
Four Gates of Lothian	Forbes Macgregor (1979)
Greyfriars Bobby	The Ampersand (1980)
Authenticated Facts relating to Greyfriars Bobby	Forbes Macgregor (1980)
Salt-sprayed Burgh	The Pinetree Press (1981)
More Macgregor's Mixture	Gordon Wright Publishing (1983)
Famous Scots	Gordon Wright Publishing (1984)

SCOTS PROVERBS

and Rhymes

Selected and compiled
with
introduction, comments
and a glossary

by

FORBES MACGREGOR

Illustrated by JOHN MACKAY

GORDON WRIGHT PUBLISHING
25 MAYFIELD ROAD, EDINBURGH EH9 2NQ
SCOTLAND

British Library Cataloguing in Publication Data

Macgregor, Forbes
    Scots Proverbs and Rhymes
    1. Proverbs, Scottish
    I. Title
    398'.9'21   PN6425 S4

    ISBN 0-903065-39-8

Typeset by Jo Kennedy
Printed and bound by Billing & Sons Ltd, Worcester.

Introduction

Every nation on earth has always had its own body of proverbs, short sayings or saws, full of meaning. Until recent times proverbs were much used but rarely written. They were the philosophy of the common people, based on generations of experience. There is no surer guide to the general character of a race than a study of its proverbs.

The Scots, as their tumultuous history shows, are a mixture of several quite different races. It is almost meaningless to speak of a typical Scotsman. There are dozens of areas in Scotland with modes of speech, traditions and outlook, peculiar to themselves. This is reflected in their proverbs and rhymes, as they have been handed down to us by the many industrious collectors and publishers. Without records we should have had very few proverbs today, for modern Scots are quite unlike their ancestors, who were reputed, not only in England, but in Europe, to have been unable to open their mouths without dropping a string of proverbs. To be fair, we must say that English members of parliament often made quite a good speech consisting of a logical procession of proverbs. Today we often wish that they would return to that picturesque brevity.

Some Scots proverbs are so very ancient that they refer to a manner of life which has totally disappeared. Both the vocabulary and the background have to be explained. Others refer to historical events and incidents which are fairly well known. Some are purely local sayings which, however, still hold human interest. Many proverbs are so self-explanatory as to be called truisms. But they also have their value in a Scottish collection.

This selection is arranged in alphabetical order. It has never been found satisfactory to arrange proverbs in categories, as many of them defy classification. A Scots-English glossary is provided.

F.M.

A bannock is a guid beast, ye may eat the guts o't on a Friday.
   Meat in Scotland meant not flesh but any kind of food, the commonest being bannocks or unleavened cakes usually of bere, pease or barley meal. There was therefore no prohibition on eating them in Lent or on Fridays.

A blate cat maks a prood moose.

A bonny bride is sune buskit
And a short horse is sune wispit.
   A pretty bride needs little decoration; a small horse little grooming.

A bonny grice maks an ugly auld soo.
   An uncomplimentary reminder to pretty girls of what old age brings.

A broken kebbuck gangs sune dune.

A cauld needs the cook as muckle as the doctor.

'A clean thing's kindly,' quo the wife when she turned her sark after a month's wear.
   This seems almost the ancestor of a Wellerism.

A crook in the Forth
Is worth an earldom in the North.
   The low lands about the river Forth were so fertile compared with the Highlands. The river Forth pursues a tortuous course with many crooks through the Carse of Stirling.

7

A croonin coo, a crawin hen, and a whistlin maid are ne'er very chancy.
>These were considered three unnatural things, girls were told.

A dish o married love richt sune grows cauld
And dozens doon to nane as folks grow auld.
>Obviously the maker of the above was beyond sentimentality.

A drap and a bite's but sma requite.
>Those who are our friends are welcome to food and drink.

A dreich drink is better than a dry sermon.
>Dreich is dry in any sense. You could take the drink or leave it, but the sermon was forced upon you.

A fair maid tocherless will get mair wooers than husbands.
>'The Tocherless Lass' puts this philosophy into song.
>Sheep and cattle I hae nane o
>No a clout to ca mine ain o
>Yet the lads are unco fain o
>To come here a-courtin me.

A fire that is all out is evil to kindle.
>Some love affairs have retained a spark or two for a long time but this is exceptional.

A fool may give a wise man a counsel.

A fool winna gie his toy for the Tower o Lunnon.
>So said a disgusted Scot on observing Charles II chasing butterflies for the amusement of the Court ladies, when the Dutch fleet lay off the Thames threatening invasion.

A gaun fit's aye gettin, were it but a thorn or a broken tae.
>The first part promises reward for enterprise and industry; but the second part warns troublemakers how they may fare.

A greedy ee ne'er got a guid pennyworth.

A guid dog ne'er barkit aboot a bane.
>Good servants are not always looking for rewards.

A guid goose may hae an ill gaislin.

A green Yule maks a fat kirkyard.
>The weather has a good deal to do with health but doctors
>have more. A young medico named Yule was most
>embarrassed when the above proverb was directed at him
>in his first practice.

A guid name is sooner tint (lost) than won.

A hairy man's a geary man
But a hairy wife's a witch.
>Rich men of the sixteenth and seventeenth centuries
>cultivated luxuriant beards. As this was the era of witch-
>hunting also, we can date this saying.

A Hawick hug.
>In Border wrestling the grip was round the waist, whereas
>in Cornwall it was above the elbows.

A head full of hair, a kirtle full of hips, a breist full of papes are
three sure marks of a daw (slut).
>An old commentary on this condemnation is that it misses
>the mark as often as it hits.

A Hieland Welcome.
>Proverbially hearty and generous, if extended to the right
>clan, or person otherwise acceptable.
>Burns wrote:
>When death's dark stream I ferry o'er
>A time that surely shall come
>In heaven itself I'll ask no more
>Than just a Hieland welcome.

A horn spune hauds nae poison.
  Humble people do not tempt poisoners.

A hungry man's meat is lang o makin ready.
  He thinks so, anyway.

A' is no gowd that glisters, nor maidens that wear their hair.
  In olden Scotland virgins went bareheaded, but so also,
  according to the cynic, did many others who had forfeited
  their privilege to dress thus.

A kiss and a drink o water mak but a wersh breakfast.
  Love in a cottage, on these terms, was evidently not
  satisfying to the practical Caledonian.

A layin hen is better than a standin mill.
  A small useful thing is better than a great useless one.

A man of five may be a fool of fifteen.

A man's a man for a' that.
  The refrain of Burns's great song of brotherhood. Among
  all differences of rank the chief merit is character.

A mile o Don's worth twae o Dee
Except for salmon, stane and tree.
  Donside is fertile, Deeside wild and forested.

A mouthfu o meat may be a tounfu o shame.
  This would be so if the food were stolen.

A muffed cat was ne'er a guid rattan taker.

A new pair o breeks will sune draw doon an auld doublet.
  Said when an old man marries a young woman.

A pun o oo is as heavy as a pun o leid.

A Scot, a craw, and a Newcastle grindstane traivel a' the warld ower.

> Scots, like crows, are great wanderers. But while some go to thieve, like the crows, many go to do honest work, like the famed grindstones.

A's fair at the ba o Scone.

> As at Jedburgh and in other handball games, there was no referee so anything went.

A schored man lives long.

> Being warned, he takes evasive action.

A Scotch warming-pan.

> Many a decent Scotch house could not afford a set of warming-pans. It was common to get a serving-lass to warm up the bed. The tale is told of a minister, visiting at a hospitable manse, who found that the serving-lass had fallen asleep in his bed. He showed his appreciation by exclaiming 'Manse o Kirkpottie, ye've wined me weel and dined me weel but this is the heicht o hospitality.'

A toom pantry maks a thriftless guid-wife.

> A wise saying for the present day. The housewife must have something to be thrifty with.

A traivelled man has leave to lie.

> Travellers' tales were acceptable as entertainment so a poetic licence was granted.

A terrier tyke and a rusty key.
Were Johnny Armstrong's Jeddart fee.

> A Border thief of that name, but not the subject of the famous ballad, was promised a free pardon on disclosing what he thought would be the best crime preventive. His reply, above, became proverbial.

A wee bush is better than nae bield.

A wee spark maks muckle wark.

A wee mouse will creep beneath a muckle corn stack.
>Said when a little woman marries a big man.

A wife is wise enough when she kens her gudeman's breeks frae her ain kirtle.
>Many a wife liked to indulge in a bit of transvestism and 'wear the breeks'.

A wilfu man maun hae his way.
>But there is an undertone which suggests that no good will come of it.

A wise man never returns by the same road if another is free to him.
>The Highlanders and Border moss-troopers kept this in mind when returning from a raid.

Absence is a shrew.

A' complain o want o siller, but nane o want o sense.
>If they had more sense they would soon have more money.

A' things anger ye and the cat breks your hert.
>A rebuke to a person who is put out by the unalterable perversity of nature.

'All new things sturts', quo the guidwife when she gaed lie wi the hired man.
>Changes are lichtsome.

Ane at a time is guid fishin.

Ane may like the kirk weel eneuch and no ride on the riggin o't.
>A canny rebuke to the over-zealous.

'Are they no a bonny pair?' as the deil said to his hoofs.

As ae door shuts anither opens.
> We are never left entirely without hope.

As auld as the hills.
> In the Highlands they add 'and the MacArthurs'.

As caller as a kail blade.
> Even in hot weather this was cool and often used to hold butter.

As daft as a yett on a windy day.

As the auld cock craws, the young ane learns.

As the day lengthens
The cauld strengthens.
> The coldest weather begins after New Year, when the days perceptibly lengthen.

As the soo fills the draff soors.
> A guest expressed his appreciation of an excellent and plentiful dinner in this way. 'There's just one serious fault your food has. It spoils my appetite.' But draff, used to feed pigs, was the refuse of grain and even pigs probably thought so.

As the wabsters, stealing through the warld.
> This was a wry punning answer to the question 'How are you getting on?' The weavers were reputed to be light-fingered, but this was probably a libel on this hard-working section of the community, inspired by political differences, for the weavers were generally Radicals, and sometimes revolutionaries.

Auld saws speak truth.

Auld sparrows are ill to tame.
> It is difficult to tame old birds, or to teach old folk new ways; though, as a point of natural interest, old rooks are more easily tamed than young ones.

13

Auld wives and bairns mak fools o physicians.

> The first from experience know what to do; the second from ignorance often pass unwittingly through great dangers.

Auld wives were aye guid maidens.

> They all say so, at any rate.

Aye keep your bonnet on: sheep's heids are best warm.

> This was said to men who impolitely kept their hats on.

Bairns and fools speak at the cross what they hear at the ingleside.

Bannocks are better than nae breid.
> Bannocks were less appetising than bread, however, being unleavened.

Be aye the thing ye would be ca'd.
> Let your conduct come up to your opinion of yourself.

Be thou weel, or be thou wae,
Thou wilt not aye be sae.

Better a moose in the pot than nae flesh.

Better bairns greet than bearded men.
> This was commonly used to justify stern measures. John Knox, on reducing Mary to tears over her non-conformity to Protestantism, quoted this proverb, substituting 'women' for 'bairns'.

Better mak your feet your friends.
> Run for your life.

Better wear shune than sheets.
> It is better to be running about healthy than bedridden, even though shoe repairs are dear.

Between Seton and the sea,
Mony a man that day shall dee.
or:

At Pinkiecleuch there shall be spilt much gentle blood that day.

Two of True Thomas's alleged prophecies which were
sure to come true over and over again, for the Lothian plain
was the cockpit of Scotland through all history. The two
battles of Dunbar (1298 and 1650) Pinkie(1560) and
Prestonpans (1745) were the major conflicts; the last two
are near Seton.

Birk will burn be it burn drawn,
Sauch will sab were it summer sawn.

Birch even if soaked in water will burn, but willow will sob
or hiss even if sawn in summer and dried until winter.

Breid's hoose is skailed never.

A house with bread is never empty of food.

Butter to butter's nae kitchen.

Used when women kiss each other, to imply that there
would be more relish in the business if one was of the
opposite sex.

Ca canny, lad, ye're but a new-come cooper.
>Go easy until you learn more about your business. This is
>a different matter from the modern sense of 'Ca canny'.

'Can do' is easily cairried aboot wi ane.
>Knowledge and skill are easily carried.

Carrick for a man, Kyle for a coo,
Cunninghame for butter and cheese,
And Gallowa for oo.
>These districts of South-west Scotland were famed for the
>above. This, we would suppose, is a Carrick proverb.
>Burns was born in Kyle, though as a youth he lived 'upon
>the Carrick border'.

Cast the cat over him.
>An old cure for a raging fever, or the ravings of a madman.

Cast a cat ower the hoose and she'll fa on her feet.
>Some people, no matter what occurs to them, never seem
>to be upset.

Cast not a cloot till May be oot.
>Don't put off any winter clothing until the hawthorn, or
>may blossom, is out; or, perhaps, until the end of May.

Changes are lichtsome, and fools like them.

Christiecleek will come to ye.
>This was a word of terror in Scotland for centuries, and
>was used effectively by mothers to frighten wayward
>children.

17

The famines, wars and anarchy of the fourteenth century caused an outbreak of cannibalism in the Highlands. One of the leaders of a cannibal gang was, inappropriately enough, named Christie, and he used to carry a large iron cleek or hook to drag down his victims. He thus earned the above name. Christie is said to have escaped the law and to have ended his life as a prosperous merchant.

Craft maun hae claes, but truth gangs nakit.

D

Ding doon the nests and the rooks will flee awa.
> The repetition of this at the Reformation led to the destruction of the abbeys by the populace.

Dinna dry up the burn because it may wet your feet.
> Don't destroy a useful thing because of a small annoyance it causes.

Dinna speak o a raip to a chiel whase faither was hanged.

Do as the coo o Forfar did.
> A woman put a newly brewed tub of beer on the doorstep to cool. It was all drunk by a passing cow whose owner was then taken to law by the 'browsterwife'. However, the Forfar magistrates found for the cow-keeper on the grounds that the cow had not sat down to drink but had taken a *deoch-an-doruis,* or door-drink (parting drink) which was always 'on the House.'

Even a haggis will run doonhill.

A soldier is not necessarily very brave who charges downhill, though this was the favourite manner of the Highlanders.

Every man has his ain bubbly-jock.

It was formerly the practice to board out daft fellows to farmers, so that they might do work and be out of mischief. A gentleman visiting one of these poor souls asked him if he were happy. He began to cry. He confessed that he had a soft bed, a full belly, and pennies for sweeties. Still he was troubled. 'O, mister, my life is made a burden to me,' he wept. At last he managed to tell his worry. 'O, sir, I'm sair hauden doon by the bubbly-jock.' It seems that the turkey-cock had taken an aversion to him and chased him at sight.

Facts are chiels that winna ding.

Facts cannot be denied.

Fair maidens wear nae purses.

Despite the reputation of the Scots for meanness, this proverb was in common usage among them when a girl offered to pay her expenses in mixed company.

Fair words winna mak the pot boil.

Fiddlers' dogs and flesh-flees come aye to feasts unca'd.
> Spoken about gate-crashers. Flesh flees are blow-flies or blue-bottles.

Fiddlers' wives and gamesters' drink are free to ilka body.
> Probably because their owners were too busy to keep an eye on them.

Fleas and girning wives are waukrife bedfellows.
> There is little sleep for the poor fellow who has to suffer either a curtain-lecture or the attentions of the indigenous *pulex irritans.*

Fools are aye fond o flittin
And wise men o sittin.

Fools and bairns shouldna see wark half-dune.

Fools look to tomorrow; wise men use tonight.

Fools mak feasts and wise men eat them.
> The Duke of Lauderdale was making a great feast in London when one of his guests very impudently said the above words. The Duke, who was a great wit, replied, 'Aye, and wise men mak proverbs and fools repeat them.'

For a hen's gerss
They'll flit i the Merse.
> The Berwickshire farm employees were addicted to changing their district every term-day on the slightest pretext. Although free range fowls enjoy an odd bit of grass, which enriches the yolks, a hen's grazing is insignificant.

Forth bridles the wild Hielandman.
> The river Forth and the Firth of Forth are so deep that they were said to keep the Highlanders from driving cattle back over them from the rich farms of the Lowlands.

Frae the greed o the Campbells
Frae the ire o the Drummonds
Frae the pride o the Grahams
Frae the wind o the Murrays,
    Good Lord deliver us!

This was the grace of an eccentric Highland laird, Maxtone of Cultoquey. He was no respecter of persons, and it is said that when visiting the Duke of Montrose, who was a Graham, he recited his customary grace, and quickly discovered the truth of his third line.

Fry stanes wi butter and the broo will be guid.

Even the most useless things can appear quite good if much is spent on them.

G

Gluttony goes hand-in-hand with drunkenness.

Gie a beggar a bed and he'll pay ye wi a loose.

Gie yer tongue mair holidays than your heid.

Giff-gaff maks guid friends.

Exchange of necessities between neighbours makes for friendship.

Guid gear gangs intae sma bouk.

Valuables are usually small, the analogy being applicable to persons. But some add to the proverb 'and sae does poison.'

21

'Hame's hamely,' quo the deil when he found himself in the Court o Session.

    Lawyers were associated with devilries.

Hang a thief when he's young and he'll no steal when he's auld.

    This is a good sample of the humour of the infamous Lord Braxfield, original of Stevenson's *Weir of Hermiston*. At the trial, in 1794, of Muir and others for alleged conspiracy, one of the accused referred to Christ as a reformer. Braxfield's reply was, 'Muckle guid he made o that! He was hangit for it!'

Half a tale is eneuch for a wise man.

Hawks winna pike oot hawks' een

He canna mak saut to his parritch.

    He cannot earn even the smallest necessity of life.

He jumped at it, like a cock at a grosset.

    He accepted the offer greedily.

He needs a lang spune that sups kail wi the deil, or a Fifer.

    Few men were considered the equal of these in cunning.

He rides wi a sark-tail in his teeth.

    Said when a newly-married man has been abroad and makes haste home. In olden times women wore a sark or chemise (Cutty-sark). One old wife interrupted her husband's pietistic speech at their Golden Wedding by remarking in a loud aside, 'Aye, John, if ye had lifted the

boards o your Bible as often as ye lifted the tail o my sark
ye wad hae been a better man today.'

He stumbles at a strae, and lowps ower a linn.
    He finds difficulties only where he wants to.

He that blaws in the stoor fills his ain een.
    He that stirs up trouble, finds himself in it.

He that eats but ae dish seldom needs the doctor.

He that gies a' his gear to his bairns
Tak up a beetle and ding oot his harns.
    This proverb is common to many nations and provides the
    main theme for 'King Lear' who did not take the proverbial
    advice. A borderer, who may have known how much
    sharper than a serpent's tooth was an ungrateful child, has
    left this rhymed epitaph:
    I, John Bell, leave here a mell, the man to fell,
    Wha gies a' to his bairns and keeps naethin to himsel.

He that invented the Maiden first hanselled it.
    The Maiden was a Scottish prototype of the guillotine, and
    was so called because it was coarsely said that though
    many men had lain with her, none had got the better of her.
    The truth of the above proverb is open to doubt, and seems
    more to satisfy a love of poetic justice than to describe the
    truth. It is supposed that the Earl of Morton, who suffered
    death by the Maiden, had introduced it shortly before. The
    same is often said, without foundation, of Dr. Guillotin.

He that's scant o breath shouldna meddle wi the chanter.
    The first steps in piping entailed using a chanter. The
    piobh mhor or great pipes were attempted later and
    required a good pair of lungs. The proverb implies that you
    should never even begin anything that you have no
    aptitude for.

He that strikes my dog would strike mysel, if he daured.

He that looks wi ae ee, and winks wi anither,
I wouldna believe him, though he was my brither.
> A childish rhyme against winkers.

He that tholes, overcomes.

He that will to Cupar, maun to Cupar.
> If a person is pig-headed, just let him go on.

He wad rake Hell for a bodle.
> Description of a miser.
> A bodle or turner was an old copper coin worth two pence Scots, or a sixth of an English penny. They were usually made in the cunzies or mints at Edinburgh or some other centre and could be stamped under licence by a nobleman. Counterfeits and spurious coinage were common despite severe penalties.
> 'Ye're like a Lauderdale bawbee,
> As bad as bad's can be.'

He would skin a loose for the talla.
> No source of gain is beneath his miserly attention.

He's an auld horse that winna nicker when he sees corn.

He's as blind as the silly blind body that his wife gart believe her gallant's horse was a milk coo sent frae her minny.
> There are many randy old songs on this theme in all languages.

He's as bold as a Lammermuir lion.
> The Lammermuir Hills is an extensive pastoral district, not 'rich in lions.'

Her auld tout will buy ye a new horn.
> A rude punning remark to a young man who felt it would be advantageous to marry an old woman. This remark was made by James VI to the young courtier about to marry Jean Lyon, Countess of Strathmore.

He's like a crane upon a pair of stilts.

> Said of any tall lank fellow. The names of cranes and herons were interchangeable in Scotland, so this proverb could apply to either. Cranes have been long extinct in Scotland where they were once abundant but the proverb may have remained in use until quite recently.

He's like the witches o Auchencraw, he'll get mair for his ill than his guid.

> A man is often granted a favour for fear of his malevolence.

Here's to you in water, I wish it were in wine.
You drink to your true love and I'll drink to mine.

His absence is good company but his backside is a cordial.

I had a wee sister, they ca'd her Peep-peep;
She waded the waters sae deep, deep, deep;
She climbed up the mountains sae hie, hie, hie;
And puir wee thing she had but yin ee.
>A star is the answer to this children's riddle.

I gied him a bonny blue nocht wi a whistle on the end o't.
>I gave him nothing worth. The Italians have a similar
>proverb, 'I paid him with a handful of flies'.

I met a man who speered at me,
Grow there berries in the sea?
I answered him by speerin again,
Is there skate on Clocknaben?
>This rhyme is a reply to inquisitive persons. Clocknaben is
>a mountain.

I ne'er lo'ed water in my shoon and my wame's made o better
leather.
>A tippler's reply when offered a drink of water.

I sat upon my houtie-croutie;
I lookit ower my rumple-routie;
And I saw John Heezlum-Peezlum
Playing on Jerusalem pipes.
>A children's rhymed riddle describing someone sitting
>looking at the moon between crossed fingers.

I will add a stone to his cairn.
>'I will testify to the virtues of the departed' is the meaning
>of this Highland proverb. In the Lowlands such an action
>had exactly the opposite meaning, and only persons
>abhorred by the populace were buried under cairns.

I, Willie Wastle, stand firm in my castle,
And a' the dogs in your toun
Canna ding Willie Wastle doon.

> This is a Scots form of 'I'm the King of the Castle'. It is
> said that this rhyme was once sent by letter challenging
> Oliver Cromwell when he was in Scotland. He im-
> mediately 'bent his cannon' on the challenger and reduced
> him.

I wish ye may hae as muckle Scots as tak ye to your bed.

> When drink began to tell, many Scots of old used to
> address the company in a rigmarole of Latin and other
> tongues. The above sarcastic wish expressed also a doubt
> whether or no the wordy one would have any coherent
> language at all before morning.

I've made a vow, and I'll keep it true,
That I'll ne'er stang man through guid sheep's woo.

> This is called the Adder's Aith. These reptiles were not
> supposed to be able to bite through woollen cloth.

I wouldna ken him if I met him in my parritch.

I would raither be your Bible than your horse.

> You overwork the latter.

If a' things are true, then that's nae lee.

> An elegant periphrasis meaning 'It's a lie'.

If a' your hums and haws were hams and haggises, the pairish
would be weel fed.

> Said to those who could not make up their minds.

If Candlemas Day be dry and fair
The hauf o winter's to come and mair;
If Candlemas Day be wet and foul
The hauf o winter's gane at Yule.

> Candlemas Day is 2 February. The rhyme tells of a
> superstition nearly two thousand years old.

If grass grows green in Janaveer
It will be the waur for't a' the year.

> Nitrogenous fertilisers have changed all that.

If I canna sew I can yerk.

> A border tailor, to eke out his earnings, took to cattle-stealing, and was being hotly pursued by an English warden, taunting him with his inefficiency as a tailor. Stung by these insults the tailor drew his bow and pinned his pursuer's thigh to the saddle, with the above observation. To yerk, or jerk, was to draw a thread smartly through tough material.

If I had a dog as daft as you, I'd shoot him.

If naebody but wise folk were to marry, the warld wad be ill peopled.

If I'm spared.

> A very common expression among the pious, and thought to be little out of the ordinary.
> An old lady, surveying a kirkyard of pleasant surroundings, remarked, 'Eh, I'd like fine to lie there some day, if I'm spared.'
> Another, bidding her tea-table friend goodnight, remarked, 'Weel, Janet, I'll see ye again next Tuesday, if I'm spared.' The other replied, a thought acidly, 'And if ye're no, I'll no expect ye.'

If ye dinna see the bottom, dinna wade.

If ye sell your purse to your wife, gie her your breeks to the bargain.

> If the wife holds the money, she rules the house.

Ilka blade o gress keps its ain drap o dew.

> Everybody has his particular business and has enough to do to attend to it.

Ill herds mak fat tods.
> The careless shepherd allows the foxes to make easy prey of his lambs.

I'll big nae sandy mills wi you.
> Ever since time was, this has been a favourite children's game. We call it building sand-castles. In this proverb it simply means, 'I won't be very friendly with you,'

I'll do as McKissoch's coo did, I'll think mair than I'll say.
> Alternatively:
> A wise old owl sat in an oak
> The more he heard the less he spoke.

I'll kiss ye behind the lug and that winna break the blood on your face.

I'll kiss ye when ye're sleeping and that'll hinder ye to dream o me when ye're deid.

I'll learn ye better manners than to bite folk in your sleep.
> This bad habit may have inspired the invention of twin beds.

It's better to hear the lark sing than the moose cheep.
> The outdoor life is the better.

It's a far cry to Lochow.
> During a battle between the Gordons and the Campbells in 1594, in which the Campbells were defeated, one of the Campbells betrayed his chief, and, as he did so, made the above remark. His meaning was that, as it was a long way to Lochow, the chief seat of the Clan Campbell, he would be safe from the anger of his people. This proverb was used to mean that it was safe to do something unlawful or sinful because there was little risk of being punished.

It's a guid goose but it has an ill gansel.
> Gansel has two meanings; a honk, or a harsh sauce made

with garlic, often used to drown the fishy, smoky flavour of solan geese or gannets which they retained even though hung in the chimney for a time before being cooked. The above proverb when applied to a woman meant she was well-favoured but had either a harsh tongue or was otherwise better avoided.

It's a lang loanin that has nae turnin.
  A change of circumstance will come sometime.

It's a sair time when the moose looks oot o the meal-kist wi a saut tear in his ee.
  When there is not enough meal to feed a mouse.

It's as easy to get siller frae a lawyer as butter frae a black dog's hause. (throat)

It's a silly hen that canna scrape for ae bird.

It's a auld tout on a new horn.
  Tell me the old, old story.

It's an ill bird that files its ain nest.
  He's a very wicked person that does evil to his own family.

It's an ugly lass that's never kissed
And a silly body that's never missed.
  A kindly proverb which our impersonal age might with advantage adopt.

'It's aye guid tae be ceevil,' quo the auld wife when she beckit to the devil.

It's far to seek and ill to find like Meg's maidenhead.
  Meg was perhaps not so worried at this libel as Chaucer's lass, 'Malkin of her maidenhead that no man desired'.

It's folly to live poor to dee rich.

It's guid to hae your cog oot when it rains kail.
>It's a good thing to have even a small share of a universal benefit.

It's ill dune to teach the cat the way to the kirn.
>From whatever motives we are actuated, we are foolish to put temptation in the way of untrustworthy persons.

It's ill makin a blawin horn oot o a tod's lug.

It's ill to tak the breeks aff a Hielandman.
>For they used to wear kilts only. You cannot take away what is not there to begin with. The forthright and eccentric C.O. of a well-known Highland regiment is said to have given a personal demonstration of the truth of this proverb, before a thousand men, during the First World War, after he had received complaints that several men were wearing trews under the kilt.

It's ill speaking between a fou man and a fasting.

It's lang or ye need cry 'Schew' to an egg.
>There's no need to worry yet or for a long time. A hen's egg, even if it hatches, takes three weeks to do so.

It's lang or four bare legs gaither heat in a bed.
>There's more to successful marriage than many think.

It's like the bairn o Blythe, it's in the hoose amang ye.
>Blythe is an isolated Lammermuir farmplace where a pregnant young woman rounded on the assembled young men, who all denied the paternity, with the 'fact that couldna ding.' 'It's in the hoose amang ye.'

It's neither by Civil Law, nor by Canon Law, but by Duns Law, that the bishops were expelled from Scotland.
>i.e. by force, for the Covenanting army assembled at Duns Law with General Leslie.

It's no easy to straucht in the aik the crook that grew in the saplin.

It's no lost what a friend gets.

It rains Jeddart staffs.
> A kind of Lochaber axe used around Jedburgh. Or, it rains cats and dogs, old wives, etc.

It stoors in an oor.
> Said in Clydesdale of very sandy soil when the wind begins to blow soil off the fields an hour after rain.

It would be a hard task to follow a black-dockit soo through a burnt muir this nicht.

Jouk and let the jaw gae by.
> Take shelter until the rough shower blows past. This was one of the first things to learn in such wild countryside as comprises much of Scotland. It also means, by easy analogy, that it is foolish to battle against what can't be avoided and will soon be past.

Keep a thing seven years and ye'll find a use for it.

Keep your ain fish-guts for your ain sea-maws.
> Charity begins at home.

Keep your breath to cool your parritch.
> Spoken to those who talked too much and out of their turn.

Keep your gab steekit when ye kenna your company.
> Be careful in talking before strangers.

Keep your mou shut and your een open.

Keep your thoomb on that.
> Cover it up discreetly. A Forfar minister, rebuking the iniquities of that worthy burgh, ended up thus: 'When Satan on the high mountain showed oor Lord the glory of all the kingdoms of the earth, ye may be sure o one thing. He keepit his thoomb on Forfar.'

Ken ye the Gordon's Gramacie?
To curse and swear and . . . and lee
That's the Gordon's Gramacie.
> We are left to guess the unprintable part of the spell-casting. Whatever it was it often amused John Gordon, Lord Kenmore, the 7th Marquis, whom Burns knew and admired. Although born nine years before Burns, he did not die until 1841, despite prophecies against the family.

Kind gallows of Crieff.
> So called because the Highlanders paid it great respect, as it had assisted at the last rites of so many of their relatives.

Kindle a candle at baith ends and it'll sune be dune.
> Bed late and rise early and you'll soon be dead.

Kindness is like cress-seed: it grows fast.

Kissing is cried down since the shaking o hands.
> When the Kirk was in its hey-day of repression in the early 18th century a ban (1727) was put on all kissing by the mouth. Even mothers were forbidden to kiss their children on a Sabbath and children born on a Sunday, and therefore presumed to have been conceived on a Sunday, were frowned on. Hand-shaking, however, was permissive.

33

Kiss my foot there's mair flesh on it.
>A good repartee, with variations, to any gallant who offered to kiss a lady's hand.

Lady, Lady Landers,
Lady, Lady Landers,
Tak your coats aboot your heid
And flee awa to Flanders.
>Children chanted this as they threw ladybirds into the air. The ladybird would then open out her wings and vanish.

Lang beards heartless,
Painted hoods witless,
Gay coats graceless,
Mak England thriftless.
>A taunting rhyme of the 14th century wars against the English.

Lang-tongued wives gang lang wi bairn.
>Those who tell everyone their plans long beforehand are unwise and invite ridicule.

Lasses are like lamb-legs: they'll neither saut nor keep.
>A pastoral version of 'Gather ye rosebuds while ye may', but in a less elevated strain.

Learn young, learn fair,
Learn auld, learn mair.

Les Ecossais sont lions dans la bataille et agneaux dans la maison.

> So said the people of Brussels at the time of Waterloo, but this proverbial compliment applied only to the Highland soldiers, or at least all those wearing the kilt (the Gordons, Black Watch and others) for this was the only way the Europeans could recognise them as 'Ecossais'. By the middle of the 19th century a large proportion of each kilted regiment was of Irish or English birth but in 1815 nearly all were of Highland origin.

Let the bell wether brak the snaw.

> The oldest and most experienced sheep in the flock, which had a bell attached about its neck, was the best to lead the flock over treacherous snow. Tried leaders are best in emergencies.

Let that flee stick to the wa; when it's dry the dirt will rub oot.

> Never mind that at present, and later we'll forget about it.

Let spades and schools do what they may
Dryfe shall tak Dryfesdale Kirk away.

> Dryfe water is a tributary of the River Annan and is notorious for great spates. Thomas the Rhymer was betting on a certainty in the above rhyme. Twice in the 17th century Dryfesdale Kirk and Kirkyard were swept away, the Kirk being finally rebuilt in Lockerbie. A macabre tale has long been current that a Dryfesdale man, going to be married, saw the coffin of his first wife washed out of the kirkyard. He interrupted his wedding long enough to rebury her. This gave rise to the rebus: 'A Dryfesdale man buried a wife and married one within the same day.'

Let us take the Pettie step to it.

> Pettie or Petty on the Nairn coast has a comparatively flat surface which may have facilitated the ancient funeral rite of running with the coffin, during which, we are told, mourners, though frequently sober, often fell.

35

'Licht's heartsome' quo the thief to the Lammas mune.

> Thieving by moonlight was common among the High-
> landers and Border moss-troopers. 'Reparabit cornua
> Phoebe' was the punning motto of the Scotts of Harden, of
> which Sir Walter Scott was a descendant. The meaning
> being that the moon would replace or renew the horns, not
> only her own, but those of the cattle stolen during the last
> moonlight period from the Scotts, either by the English or
> Scottish neighbours.

Lift me up and I'll tell you more.

> A stranger came upon this line carved on a great stone in a
> moor. He gathered a number of local helpers to help him
> turn over the stone, and, expecting to find treasure, paid
> them all handsomely. His helpers laughed knowingly
> when, on the other side of the stone, there appeared the
> line:
>> Lay me doon as I was before.

Licht suppers mak lang days.

> The Scots were often forced to make a virtue of necessity.

Like Moses' breeks—neither shape, form nor fashion.

> In the old illustrated Bibles, Moses was often shown
> dressed in a very extraordinary fashion. The comparison
> was applied to any oddly-made article.

Like the drinkers o Sisterpath Mill.

> These Berwickshire men, inspired by what Dr. Henderson
> calls 'determined sociality' sat down to drink when a hen
> was set upon a clutch of eggs and did not rise until the
> chicks were running about the house.

Like the Laird of MacFarlane's geese, they liked their play
better than their meat.

> James VI, at dinner with the MacFarlane chief on an
> island in Loch Lomond, had noticed the geese chasing one
> another on the loch; but the bird served for dinner was so

tough as to draw forth the above remark from the waggish monarch.

Little kens the auld wife as she sits by the fire.
Hoo blaws the wind in the Hurly-Burly Swire.
 A witch in Macbeth used hurly-burly figuratively to mean a battle. The Swire above is a windswept gully high above the sources of the Tweed and Annan and Clyde, which 'a' rise oot o ae hillside.' The proverb is aimed at arm-chair critics.

Little's the licht will be seen on a mirk nicht.

Love and raw pease are two ill things, one breaks the heart, the other bursts the belly.

Macfarlane's lantern.
 A proverbial name for the moon, which lit the wild Macfarlanes upon their excursions.

Macgregor as the rock
Macdonald as the heather.
 This is the translation of an ancient provocative Gaelic proverb which probably expressed the view that the Macdonalds, as descendents of the Scottish Gaels, were comparative newcomers to the land compared with the Macgregors, who traced their descent (always a touchy matter with the Highlanders) to the aboriginal Picts.

Maidens' bairns are weel guided.
 Being of those 'whose habitation is in the air, are the best-conditioned Creatures imaginable.'

Maidens should be mim till they're mairret then they may burn kirks.

'Mair haste, the waur speed,'
Quo the wee tailor to the lang threid.

Maist things hae a sma beginnin.

Mak a kirk or a mill o't.
> Do as you please with it.

Making a rope of sand.
> Before the days of glass fibre this was thought impossible.
> Michael Scott the magician and Black Duncan Campbell
> of Glenorchy didn't have the technique, for traditionally,
> both their attempts failed.

Many men speak o my meikle drink, but few o my sair thirst.
> Burns sublimates this in:
> What's done we partly may compute
> We ken not what's resisted.

March dust and March wun'
Bleach as weel as simmer's sun.
> Clydesdale again. Foresters say that such conditions are
> as hard on vegetation as the Sahara.

Mealy-moo'd maidens stand lang at the mill.
> This seems like an indictment of pre-marital intercourse.

Mennans are better than nae fish.

Moosie, moosie, come to me,
The cat's awa frae hame.
Moosie, moosie, come to me,
I'll use ye kind, and mak ye tame.
> An invitation never accepted by 'moosie'.

38

Monday's bairn is fair o face;
Tuesday's bairn is fu o grace;
Wednesday's bairn is a bairn o wae;
Thursday's bairn has far to gae;
Friday's bairn is lovin, forgivin;
Saturday's bairn warks hard for a livin;
But the bairn that is born on the Sabbath day
Is lively and bonny and wyce and gay.

Mony ane's deen ill wi vreet.
>   This, in Buchan dialect, belittles literacy on the ground
>   that many a person has committed crimes with the aid of
>   writing.

Mony haws, mony snaws.
>   In England, this rhyme was:
>   Many haws, many sloes
>   Many cold toes.
>   But this is to confuse cause and effect, for the abundance of
>   haws and sloes depends on factors during flowering. For
>   haws, which bloom in early June, there should be abun-
>   dance of fertilising insects, and for sloes, which bloom in
>   mid-April before the leaf, there must be no frost.

More land is won by the lawyer with the ramskin than by the
Andrea Ferrara with his sheepskin handle.
>   i.e. by parchment deeds than by deeds of war.

Muck is the mither o the meal kist.
>   This was in the days before the chemical fertilisers.

Muckle-mou'ed Meg.
>   This epithet has been applied to Mons Meg, the great
>   cannon in Edinburgh Castle, but it was the nickname of
>   Agnes Murray, daughter of Gideon Murray of Elibank.
>   Murray captured William Scott, son of the notorious
>   Watty Scott of Harden, and gave this handsome young
>   man this choice: the gallows or Agnes.

He chose Agnes.

From this 'shot-gun' wedding arose the family to which Sir Walter Scott belonged. In ancient times women could save condemned men by offering to marry them, but this was not recognised in the law of England.

Muckle to mak a wark aboot, a deid cat in your parritch.

A sarcastic remark to fuss-pots.

Multiplication is vexation,
Division is as bad;
The rule of three it vexes me,
And practice drives me mad.

This rhyme was commonly printed by schoolchildren upon their arithmetic books.

Another favourite rhyme was:
.. .. .. is my name,
Scotland is my nation;
... is my hame,
And H ... my destination.

The blanks were filled in according to the whims of the writer.

My coo's bulled and my soo's branned and I'm in grand fettle mysel.

This was the apparently innocent reply of a young widow cottager of Lochmaben to the farmer who asked her how she was getting on.

Nae gairdener ever lichtlied his ain leeks.
No man speaks ill of what he values most.

Naebody is riving your claes to get ye.

Naebody's nails can reach the length o Lunnon.
When the Government was in London (after the Union of 1707) at least this did away with the bribery and cajolery that previously went on in Edinburgh.

Naething like being stark deid.
Spoken with malicious satisfaction upon hearing of the death of an enemy.

Naething to be done in haste but grippin fleas.

Ne'er find faut wi my shune, unless ye pay my soutar.
Don't criticise something outwith your knowledge and concern.

Ne'er let your feet run faster than your shune.
Don't outstrip your resources.

Ne'er look for a wife until ye hae a hoose and a fire to put her in.
The misplaced phrase suggests that the giver of this advice was also 'het at hame', i.e. on ill terms with his wife.

Ne'er marry a widow unless her first husband was hanged.

Ne'er misca a Gordon in the raws of Stra'bogie.
Don't speak badly of a man among his friends. The Gordons were the principal clansmen about Strathbogie, in north-west Aberdeenshire.

Ne'er speak ill o them whase breid ye eat.

Ne'er tak a stane to brak an egg when ye can dae it wi the back o your knife.

> To bring a great force against a contemptible obstacle only invites ridicule.

Neither sae sinful as to sink nor sae holy as tae soom.

> This proverb, quoted by Cheviot, is the wrong way about. Floating proved a witch's guilt, and she was pulled ashore to be burned; sinking proved her innocence but did not help her much either.

Nineteen nay-says o a maiden is half-a-grant.

Nipping and scarting is Scotch folks wooing.

> A gentle lover, who had observed all the proprieties to his fair Delia, said, on becoming betrothed: 'Weel, onywey, I've aye been ceevil to ye.' 'Aye, senselessly ceevil, ye muckle gowk,' she replied.

O, wad some power the giftie gie us
To see oorsels as ithers see us!

> A well-known wish of Burns, which is not likely to be granted. It has become proverbial and is one of the few Scots proverbs still much used.

O bairns' gifts ne'er be fain,
Nae suner they gie than they tak it again.

Out o Davie Lindsay into Wallace.

> *Davie Lindsay* and *Wallace* were two books popular in Scotland during the 16th and 17th centuries, tales of humour and adventure.
> This proverb meant that a boy was advancing in his schooling.

Ower guid for banning and ower bad for blessing.

> Banning was cursing in the old religious sense. The proverb was applied to Rob Roy's character which more than most of humanity partook of the mixed nature of the curate's egg.

Pigs may whistle but they have an ill moo for it.

> Not just another injustice to the 'Irish nightingales' but a warning to those who attempt any feats beyond their powers.

Powder me weel and keep me clean,
I'll carry a ba' to Peebles Green.

> This was said about Mons Meg, the great cannon in Edinburgh Castle. But on one occasion long ago, after the cannon had been fired in salute, the ball was retrieved from Wardie Moor only two miles away, so we are justified in doubting whether Meg could have reached Peebles, twenty miles away.

Put twa pennies in a purse and they'll creep thegither.

Rain, rain, rattlestanes,
Dinna rain on me,
But rain on Johnny Groat's hoose
Far ower the sea.

> Chanted by children during a heavy shower of sleet or hail.

Raise nae mair deils than ye can lay.

> This refers to the ancient belief in the power to raise spirits out of the earth by magic, as described in the *Odyssey*, the *Book of Kings*, and elsewhere. But the proverb probably means nothing more than, 'Don't start anything you can't stop.'

Rattan and moose,
Lea' the puir woman's hoose;
Gang awa ower to the mill,
And there ane and a' ye'll get your fill.

> Those whose homes were infested by rodents wrote this
> doggerel on the wall, or on a piece of paper, where the
> animals could see it and, unless illiterate, read it.

Rise when the day daws,
Bed when the nicht fa's.

> This proverb dates from a more Arcadian age than the
> present.

Rodden tree and reid threid
Put the witches to their speed.

> These, among such articles as amber beads and horse-
> shoes, were supposed to prevent the attentions of witches
> and warlocks.

Ru'glen Marriage.

> Civil marriage was easily contracted in old Scotland
> without papers etc. The Kirk required more formalities but
> supplied documentary evidence. In Rutherglen a quick
> and cheap way to obtain a 'certificate' was to have a friend
> inform the Sheriff that a marriage without legal banns had
> been made. The Sheriff fined the parties 5s. and the receipt
> was accepted as a marriage certificate.

Scorn not the bush that bields ye.

Scotch washing.
> Clothes were tramped on in a wooden tub of soapy water usually on the public drying-green attached to every town; Glasgow Green or Calton Hill, Edinburgh, for example. A popular coloured postcard of Edwardian times was of Scots lassies in plaids doing a Scotch washing and displaying an immodest length of shapely leg.

Seagull, seagull, sit on the sand,
It's never good weather when you're on the land.
> Yet the black-headed gull spends much of its year far inland, nesting and feeding. The common gull, or herring-gull, is probably meant in this proverb.

Seek never het fire under cauld ice.
> Though it is unwise to go by appearances, some things are just as they seem. This very old proverb is worked into the ballad of Johnnie Armstrong, where he realises he shall have no mercy from James V, and addresses James thus:
>> To seek het water beneath cauld ice
>> Surely it is greit folie
>> I hev socht grace at a graceless face
>> And there is nane for my men and me.

Set a stoot hert to a stey brae.
> The harder the task, the more determination is needed.

Sic things maun be if ye sell ale.
> This was the complacent reply of the innkeeper's wife when he caught her with the exciseman.

Some hae meat that canna eat,
And some wad eat that want it;
But we hae meat, and we can eat,
For which the Lord be thankit.

> The Covenanters' 'Grace before Meat', a favourite with
> Burns and grown proverbial. 'Want' in the second line
> means 'lack', not 'desire'.

Sorrow and ill weather come unca'd.

> These two evade all attempts at planning.

Speak o the deil and he'll appear.

> Said, as a joke, when someone appears of whom the
> company has been talking.

Speak weel o the Hielands, but dwell in the Laigh.

> Those who inhabited the Moray Coast, or Laigh o Moray,
> were wisely advised neither to invite the hostility nor to
> seek the hospitality of their turbulent Highland neigh-
> bours.

Spunky, Spunky, ye're jumpin licht,
Ye'll ne'er tak hame the schule-bairns richt,
But through the rough moss and ower the hag-pen,
Ye droon the ill anes in your watery den.

> A rhyme to intimidate ill-doers, about the Spunky, or Will
> o Wisp.

Sticks and stanes may brak my banes,
But names'll never hurt me.

> This chant is still used by schoolchildren as a reply to
> abusive language.

Steek your een and open your mou
And see what the King'll send ye.

> This rhyme is spoken in fun to boys and girls when
> someone wishes to put a tasty bite into their mouth. It
> sometimes ends in a practical joke.

47

Sunny, sunny shooer
Come in for hauf-an-hour,
Gar a' the hens cour,
Gar a' the hares clap,
Gar ilka wife o Lammermuir
Put on her kail-pat.

> A Berwickshire rhyme graphically describing the effects of a heavy shower. The shepherd's wife heats up the kail, or broth, because she shall soon have her husband home, drenched, from the bare hillside.

Suppers kill mair than doctors cure.

> But these were the suppers of a Gargantuan age.

Sunday comes seldom aboon the Pass o Ballybrough.

> The ancient Highlanders were not Sabbatarians until after the missionaries had been at work, when you could hear such conversations as:
> Sassenach visitor: This is a grand Sabbath day, Donald.
> Donald: This is not a day to be speaking of days, whatever.
> or
>
> Lowland minister (excusing himself for enjoying a Sunday stroll): Did not our Lord walk abroad on the Sabbath?
> Highland elder: Ay, and I never thocht ony the mair o him for that.

Sweet in the bed and sweir up in the morning was ne'er a gude housewife.

Tak awa Aiberdeen, and twal mile roond, and far are ye?
>There would be, in the opinion of the Aberdonians, very little worth in the North if Aberdeen and its fertile hinterland were removed.

Tak a lass wi a tear in her ee.

Tak a piece, your teeth's langer than your beard.
>A kindly excuse for giving a child an extra titbit.

Tak yer ain tale hame.
>Take the advice yourself. At the Union of 1707 Lord Seafield, the Chancellor, objected to his brother, Colonel Ogilvie, dealing in cattle as unbecoming to his rank. Ogilvie replied, 'Tak yer ain tale hame. I sell nowt, but ye sell nations.'

Tak your ain will o't as the cat did o the haggis, just ate it and then creepit into the bag.
>A Parthian shot at those who won't listen to reason.

Tammy Norrie o the Bass
Canna kiss a bonny lass.
>This rhyme describes the puffins which nest on the Bass Rock. They have a parrot-like beak. But a Tammy Norrie is any shy, awkward fellow.

Tell me where the flea may bite
And I'll tell you where love may light.

Thanks winna feed the cat.
>This is a boorish speech, and is much on a line with the

Highlander's remark when the tourist admired the magnificent scenery. 'Maybe aye, but ye canna fatten the coos on't.' The Scots were not fond of bombastic language, and took some delight in deflating it with such unsentimental remarks.

That was langsyne, when geese were swine
And turkeys chewed tobacco,
And sparrows bigget in auld men's beards,
And mowdies delved potatoes.

This was considered a good reply to a scarcely credible statement.

The aik, the ash, the elm-tree,
They are hanging a' three.

Under the harsh forest laws of mediaeval Scotland, which of course applied only to territory under feudal rule, it was a capital crime to mutilate those trees.

The Auld Man o Embro.

Public conveniences were unknown in old Edinburgh or elsewhere, although there were noisome areas off the Canongate and Cowgate dedicated to the easing of Nature. As civilisation crept on, an old man provided with a very long and wide 'maxi', which concealed two wooden tubs suspended from a dairymaid's yoke, went around the area of the Law Courts crying 'Wha wants me?'

In June 1792, when political feeling ran high, Henry Dundas was caricatured by James Gillray and John Kay in the above role, because of his corrupt political practices.

The best-laid schemes o mice and men
Gang aft a-gley.

This is perhaps the most universally quoted of Burns' lines, though not always spoken in Scots.

The breath o a fause friend's waur than the fuff o a weasel.

The most ferocious creature, weight for weight, is the weasel. Before attacking a man it squeals, then fuffs. This was accounted an odious noise, but had the merit of being without deceit.

The coo that's first up gets the first o the dew.

The corbie says unto the craw,
'Johnny fling your plaid awa.'
The craw says unto the corbie,
'Johnny, draw your plaid aboot ye.'
> If the raven calls first in the morning, the day will be fine; if
> the carrion crow, then wet. With the present scarcity of
> ravens, few can benefit by these meteorological portents.

The deil's aye guid to his ain.
> A jocular expression nowadays, but in former times it was
> believed that Auld Nick had power to provide for his
> adherents.

The emot bites sairer than the clok.
> The ant-bite is worse than the beetle's. This probably
> means that it is dangerous to interfere with a man seriously
> engaged in business.

The fish that sooms in a dub will aye taste o mud.

The gravest fish is an oyster;
The gravest bird's an owl;
The gravest beast's an ass;
And the gravest man's a fule.

The Gudeman's croft.
> A small plot of the best land near a village, put aside for the
> Devil and never to know the plough. This was an ancient
> Celtic custom commemorated in old French, 'Et tous ces
> lieux sont Artus de Bretagne,' such fairy ground being
> under the protection of the immortal Arthur.

The gule, the Gordon and the hoodie craw.
The three worst things that Moray ever saw.
> The gule is the yellow corn-cockle, a bad weed. The
> Gordons and the carrion crows also annoyed the Men o
> Moray.

51

The gustin bane o Kirkmahoe.

> There is a long story and a ballad (by Cunningham) about this curious custom in a Dumfriesshire village. The people are said to have been so poor that they could not afford meat for the broth but hired a bone, at a halfpenny for a few dips, to give it a flavour.
>
> This is probably a 'made' story, libellous. Anyone who wanted to start a riot in Kirkmahoe chanted this couplet:
>
> > Wha'll buy me? Wha'll buy me?
> > Three plumps and a wallop for a bawbee.

The King lies doon,
Yet the warld rins roond.

> No man is indispensable.

The lasses o Exmagirdle
May very weel be din
From Michaelmas till Whitsunday
They never see the sun.

> Ecclesmagirdle is a small village on the north side of the Ochils and consequently is deprived of sunshine for months during the winter. There are parts of Glen Lyon where this also happens.

The lasses o Lauder are mim and meek
The lasses o the Fanns smell o peat reek
The lasses o Gordon canna sew a steek
But weel can they sup their crowdie
The lasses o Earlston are bonnie and braw
The lasses o Greenlaw are black as a craw
But the lasses o Polwart are best o them a
And gie plenty wark to the howdie.

> Composed by a west Berwickshire amateur.

The lazy lad maks the stark auld man.

> Stark means strong, not naked. In the parallel Gaelic proverb the old man is *brisg* or brisk in English. There are no Scots or Gaelic proverbs condemning laziness in youth.

52

The light infantry of Satan.
> The fairies.

The Lindsays in green should never be seen.
> So many green-robed Lindsays were killed in a battle near Brechin that they avoided this colour as a battle-dress.

The loodest bummer's no the best bee.

The mair mischief, the better sport.
> When old Simon Fraser, Lord Lovat, was awaiting execution in London for his part in the '45, he heard that a scaffolding for spectators had given way, killing and injuring many who had gathered to see him executed. With no show of sympathy, he coolly quoted the above.

The men o the East
Are pykin their geese,
And sendin their feathers here-awa, there-awa.
> Children used to sing this at the onset of snow.

The muirhen has sworn by her teuch skin
She ne'er shall eat o the carle's win.
> The waterhen or moorhen was supposed never to eat of field crops.

The nearer the grave, the greedier.

The next time ye dance in the dark, ken wha ye tak by the hand.
> Perhaps, like Donne, the imprudent dancer 'longed to talk with some old lover's ghost.'

The peesweep aye cries farrest frae its ain nest.
> Most people, however naive they appear, are cunning enough to mislead those who are trying to get the better of them.

The proof o the pudden's in the preein o't.

The scourging of a nine-gallon tree.
    Broaching a firkin of ale and drinking it all at a sitting.

The siller penny slays mair souls than the nakit sword slays bodies.

The soutar gae the soo a kiss
'Grumph!' quo she, 'it's for a birse.'
    A birse was a bristle used to stiffen thread when sewing leather. An ugly woman often suspects the motives of a wooer.

The robin and the lintie,
The laverock and the wren,
Them that herries their nests
Will never thrive again.
    These four sweet singers are the most innocent of birds.

The tae hauf the warld thinks the tither hauf daft.

The tod ne'er kills the lamb except at a distance frae his ain hole.
    A fox will travel over a parish rather than kill near his den, as he knows that this would lead to his destruction. Some persons also do evil far from home and are all innocence to their neighbours. This proverb could have been applied very fittingly to the behaviour of Charles II, who liked everyone to be happy in his Court but caused 18,000 persons to be butchered in Scotland during his reign.

The water will ne'er waur the widdie.
    A man that is born to be hanged will never be drowned.

The wife's ae dochter and the cottar's ae coo
The tane's ne'er weel and the tither's ne'er fu.
    A warning to avoid pampered cattle.

The willing horse is aye wrocht tae daith.

The wrang side o a bannock to a Menteith.

The betrayer of Wallace was his own close friend Graham
of Menteith. For centuries this abhorrent crime was kept
green by unfailingly serving a Menteith with a bannock
wrong side up. But, even as late as the publication of the
Imperial Gazetteer of Scotland, a century ago, though
there is a long article on Menteith, including history, no
reference is made to this supreme treachery, a conspicuous
omission.

Them that's brocht up like beggars are aye warst to please.

There came never luck o a hen's flichter or a hure's lauchter.
There was always mischief brewing somewhere in the
vicinity.

There was never a caik
But there was a maik
But the caik o Tollishill.

This rhyme originated in the following way. The farmer's
wife of Tollishill in Lauderdale repaid the Earl of Lauderdale for the life-long remission of her rental by baking a cake
full of new-minted guineas and taking it to him when he was a
prisoner in the Tower.

There ne'er was a bad, but there micht be a waur.
It is hard to say whether or not this is a comforting thought.

There was little meat and muckle mirth
At little Bauldy's wedding.

Recorded by Dr. George Henderson. A common remark at
Berwickshire weddings when the fare was scant. A similar
sarcasm used in the fisher town of Newhaven was, 'If it's to
be a wedding, let it be a wedding. Bring oot anither herring.'

There was mair lost at Sherramuir whaur the Hielandman lost his
faither and his mither and a gude buff belt worth baith o them.
Quoted when someone has a trifling loss.

There's an act in the Laird o Grant's court that no abune eleven speak at once.

A sarcasm aimed at interrupters.
Some of the television audience participation programmes should apply this act.

There's aye some water whaur the stirkie droons.

There must be some cause for a great fault or misfortune, no matter though people may try to explain it all away.

There's a piece wad please a Brownie.

The Brownie, or domestic fairy drudge, was always left a delicacy at night in the form of a bowl of cream or a bannock buttered or spread with honey. But it was provoking disaster to leave a Brownie anything other than this.

There was ne'er a guid toon but there was a dub at the end o't.
More lyrically, no rose without a thorn.

There was never a goose without a gander.

An encouragement to unattractive would-be wooers of either sex.

There's as guid cheese in Choicelee
As ever was chowed wi chafts
And the cheese o Cheshire
Is nae mair like the cheese o Choicelee
Than chalk's like cheese.

Choicelee is a farm near Duns, Berwickshire. Cromwell's troops are said to have given Choicelee the above reputation about fifty years before the famous Dunlop cheese was first made in Ayrshire.

There's nae airn sae hard but rust will fret it;
There's nae cloth sae fine but moths will eat it.

There seems to be a touch of malice in this proverb, as if the person quoting it were somehow rejoicing in mortality and, like John Knox, holding up a death's-head for all to see. A

56

similar proverb which I have heard is, 'There was naething made yet but it wad brek.' This is the savage spirit of many of the 'Guid and Godlie Ballants' of the 17th century.

'There's baith meat and music here,' quo the dog when he ate the bagpipes.
This comical proverb was often repeated by those who were invited to an entertainment and found refreshments as well as musicians.

There's nae guid speaking o the Laird within his ain bounds.
The devil should never be referred to in haunted places.

There's naething got by delay but dirt and lang nails.

There's nocht sae queer as folk.
Even in the days before psycho-analysis, the heart of man was known to be more unfathomable than all other natural phenomena.

There's nocht for it but the twa thoombs.
A unique proverb, made during the war of 1914-18 by a Gordon Highlander. The sanitary authorities having failed to de-louse or de-flea the garments of the battalion, this canny lad made the above remark, referring to the primitive but sure method of killing fleas and lice by crushing them between the thumb-nails.

They craw crouse that craw last.

They hae need o a canny cook that hae but ae egg to their denner.

They that are born on Hallowe'en ken mair than ither folk.
The fairies abroad that night whisper secrets to them.

They tint never a coo that grat for a needle.
Those that weep for a trifling loss never suffered a great one.

They wha pay the piper hae a richt tae ca' the tune.

They wha hae a guid Scots tongue in their heid are fit to gang ower the warld.

> The implication here is that they will always find someone who can understand them, i.e. a fellow-Scot.

They wha stey in gless hooses shouldna thraw stanes.

> This proverb is attributed to James VI and I, who is said to have replied in these words to Buckingham, who was complaining of the London Scots breaking his windows. It was known to the King that the young Duke had previously, in a frolic, broken the Scots' windows.

They're tarred a' wi ae stick.

> It was the habit to mark sheep with tar to distinguish the ownership, the proverb could apply to people who were alike in bearing a common vice, the brand of Auld Nick.

They're fremit friends that canna be fashed.

> They're strange friends who cannot be bothered.

This is like the fiddler o Chirnside's breakfast,
A' pennyworths together.

> The fiddler sent his small son with sevenpence to give this order:
> A pennyworth o tea
> A pennyworth o sugar
> Three penny loaves
> A pennyworth o butter
> And a pennyworth o he-herring
> For my father likes milts.

This is the tree that never grew
This is the bird that never flew
This is the bell that never rang
This is the fish that never swam.

> A description of the armorial bearings of the City of Glasgow, whose full motto is 'Let Glasgow Flourish ... by the preaching of the Word.'

Think mair than ye say.

Three failures and a fire make a Scotsman's fortune.
    A libel sometimes applied to other nations.

Times tries a', as winter tries the kail.
    The hardy kail, or borecole, was for long the only
vegetable in the Lowlands of Scotland. Indeed, in the
Highlands they did not relish the refinement of kail, but ate
boiled nettles. The point of the proverb is that the kail was
unpalatable until after it had suffered frost, which, however, often killed some of it. So with people: if they could
survive the trials of life, without being embittered, they
were a great asset to humanity and a credit to their kind.

Tip when ye like ye shall lamb wi the lave.
    At a drinking-party this meant that like the parable of the
labourers, whenever you started it was 'equal shares' at
the end. But ewes are under no such compulsion and must
lamb after their natural term of gestation, whether in
January or June.

To be under Bowmaker's purgative.
    Means to make a weak excuse.
    In 1498, Bowmaker, captured by the English the day
following the battle, denied having fought against them,
saying he had been under a purgative, and could not have
been conveniently under arms.

To burke.
    To strangle or suffocate as Burke and Hare did in the
notorious murders around 1827.

To cast a leglingirth.
    This is a metaphor drawn from the shepherd's life. The
leglingirth was the lowest hoop on a pail, for milking ewes.
If it became loose and fell off, the milk ran out. But in a
figure of speech it meant having an illicit love affair.

To 'lift' a young lady.

> To request her to dance. At a ball the M.C. saw that the sisters MacFarlane who each weighed around fifteen stone were not dancing. He quizzed the men: 'Lads, are nane o ye gaun to lift the Miss MacFarlanes?'

To send round the fiery peat.

> This was done on the Borders to summon the clans or family adherents. In the Highlands the expression was 'the fiery cross', but it was never sent round alight: one end was charred black, the other reddened with blood, to symbolise fire and slaughter.

Truth and honesty keep the croon o the causey.

> The 'croon o the causey' was the highest and driest part of the street. When the gutters were so filled with filth, and never flushed until heavy rain came, there was naturally much competition for the 'croon o the causey'. The most respectable citizens generally insisted upon walking there.

Truth will stand when a'thing's failin.

> This noble proverb is found in 'Caller Herrin', written by Lady Caroline Nairne about the Newhaven fisherwomen.

Turning the riddle.

> An old method of finding a thief by 'magic', using a riddle, scissors and a string.

Tweed said to Till,
'What gars ye rin sae still?'
Till said to Tweed,
'Though ye rin wi speed,
And I rin slaw,
Yet where ye droon ae man
I droon twa.'

> When the Scots retired in small companies from Flodden Field after their defeat, twice as many were drowned in the Till as in the Tweed: the still waters of the narrow Till deceived many, while the wide and brawling but shallower Tweed claimed few victims.

60

Upaland folk hae muirland manners.
> Upaland or Upon-land folk meant country folk.

'Upon my ain expenses', as the man built the dyke.
> A quotation from a Macaronic inscription in the church-yard of Foot Dee or Fitty, Aberdeen.
> 'I, John Moody, cives Abredonensis,
> Builded this kerk-yerd, o Fitty, upon my ain expenses.'

Use of hand is father of lear.
> First learn to use your hands; that opens the way to other knowledge.

Want o wit is waur than want o gear.

Wattie Ross o the Crawbutt
Never took a supper
But just a chack o cheese and breid
And a lang waught o porter.
> The substitute for supper was more than adequate, for this Berwickshire man grew in girth until he featured in another rhyme.
> O Wattie Ross pu up your breeks
> Nor let your kyte shine through the steeks
> Your shop-door hangs so low, man.

Weary fa the Trot o Turry.
> The Covenanters got the worst of it at a skirmish near Turriff, Aberdeenshire, and it was commemorated in the saying.

Weel kens the moose that the cat's oot o the hoose.

Weel saipet is hauf shaven.

We'll a gang thegither like the folk o the Shiels
And defy the bogles, the ghaists and the deils.
> Berwickshire used to have many areas of heath and moss close to the arable, and these places were associated with the above agents. Country folk, returning from social gatherings late into the night, banded together and whistled or sang to keep their courage up as they passed these haunts.

We'll wet thoombs on that.
> Swear solemnly to keep faith.

We're to learn while we live.
> Often said in irony.

We shall see at Doomsday whose backside is blackest.
> Charles II, wearied by political arguments, quoted this.

Wha daur bell the cat?
> This is about the best known of the Scots proverbs. At a meeting of mice, when they were discussing how to deal with the cat, a young mouse said that a bell should be hung round the cat's neck, then all might hear him coming. An old mouse rather spoiled this clever scheme by asking, 'Who will bell the cat?'
>
> In Scottish history there is a story that, at a meeting of nobles to discuss how to deal with Cochrane, the favourite of James III, some suggested seizing and hanging Cochrane. Lord Gray remarked, 'Well said, but who will bell the cat?' Douglas, Earl of Angus, said that he would do it, and soon after he hanged Cochrane and a number of the King's servants over Lauder Bridge.

'What's no in the bag will be in the broo,' as the Hielandman said when he dirked the haggis.

What fizzes in the mou winna fill the wame.
>Tasty food is not always best, and this principle applies to all attractive things.

When a' men speak, nae man hears.

When Cheviot ye see pit on his cap
O rain ye'll hae a wee bit drap;
When Ruberslaw draws on his coul
Wi rain the burns will a' be full.
>A Border proverb of the weather. The lower the clouds, the more rain.

When the bag's fu the drone gets up.
>An analogy between bagpipes and boozing.

When the mune's on her back
Gae mend your shoon and sort your thack
When roond the mune there is a brugh
The weather will be cauld and reuch.
>The first part of the rhyme is as likely to be wrong as right because the moon must go through its phases whatever the weather. The second part which tells of the ring round the moon, indicating much moisture in the atmosphere, has more logic about it.

When Tweed and Pausayl meet at Merlin's grave
Scotland and England will one monarch have.
>This smacks of True Thomas, and the truth of it has been vouched for by Robert Chambers, a native of Peebles who records that on that date, when James VI was crowned King of England, the Tweed was in such an unprecedented spate that its waters joined the Powsail or Pausayl Burn under the very hawthorn tree which was reputed to mark the grave of Myrdinn or Merlin, the prince who went mad after the slaughter of his people at Arderyd in 573 A.D.

When Yule comes
Dule comes,
Cauld feet and legs;
When Pasch comes
Grace comes,
Butter, milk and eggs.

Pasch is Easter, and rhymes with grace.

Where there's muckle courtesy there's little kindness.

Whistling amang the tenantry.

This was the detestable passing of information to the factor about improvements made by a neighbour, so that his rent could be raised. Farmers were completely at the mercy of their factors and landlords, holding leases only from year to year. Great improvements followed the granting of longer leases, usually from nineteen years upwards.

Whoredom and grace will not bide in one place.

Yet Burns said that he had discovered that religious women could be whores.

'Willie Burd, Willie Burd, here's a bum-bee.'
Quo the miser o Reston to his little Willie.

When his son asked him for a bawbee (halfpenny) he skipped up and down waving his arms and buzzing to imitate a bum-bee, hoping to take his son's attention off the question of money. The origin of 'bawbee' has been much disputed but Professor Gregory Smith had no doubt it derived from the mint-master who first produced them, Alexander Orrock of Sillebawby.

Wise men buy and sell, and fools are bought and sold.

Wives maun hae their wills while they live for they may mak nane when they dee.

This was the state of things before the 'Married Women's Act' early in the century. Many a young scapegrace enriched himself by marrying a young heiress and afterwards got rid of her. This was one of the chief scandals of the 'Gretna Green' runaway wedding.

Wood in a wilderness, moss in a mountain and wit in a poor man's pow are little thought of.

Words are but wind but dunts are the devil.
    Assault is worse than abuse.

Wrang compt is nae payment.

Ye are like the cat, ye love fish but not to wet your feet.

Ye breed o the leek, ye hae a white heid and a green tail.
    This was a rebuke to old men who were full of bawdy talk.

Ye breed o Leddy Mary, when ye're gude ye're ower gude.
    A drunk man prayed to Our Lady to help him mount his horse. After many attempts, preceded by as many petitions, his piety was doubly rewarded. He cleared his mount and landed on the other side.

Ye breed o oor laird, ye'll dae nae richt and ye'll tak nae wrang.

Ye breed o Saughton swine, your neb's never oot o an ill turn.
    You are never happy unless you are uprooting something and making trouble.

Ye canna gaither berries aff a whinbush.
    Don't go to ill-tempered people for favours.

65

Ye canna hae mair o a soo than a grumph.

Ye canna mak a silk purse oot o a soo's lug.

Ye canna put an auld heid on young shouthers.

Ye come o the MacTaks, but no o the MacGies.
>Those clans are found all over the world; the saying means, 'You're greedy.'

Ye cut lang whangs aff ither folk's leather.
>You make very free with other people's property.

Ye didna draw sae weel when my mare was in the mire.
>You did not help me in my trouble as much as I now help you in yours.

Ye found it where the Hielandman found the tongs.
>You stole it: the Hielandman had a reputation for thieving, not undeserved.
>This proverb recalls a notice in a certain golf course, 'Players are requested not to pick up lost balls until they have stopped rolling.'

Ye glower like a cat oot o a whin bush.
>These were wildcats, as are intended in the motto of the clan Chattan, 'Touch not a cat bot a glove.'

Ye hae a streak o carl hemp in ye.
>The carl hemp was the main stem or toughest fibre of the hemp. Burns uses this phrase to mean great resolution.

Ye hae gotten to your English.
>When a Highlander, addressing his opponent in argument, wished to satisfy his self-esteem he aspired to grand-iloquent though often uncouth English. The above remark, which became proverbial, was judged to be the most aggravating reply that could be readily made, reminding the eloquent one that he was out of his element in attempting the mastery of a foreign tongue.

Ye hae little need o the Campsie wife's prayer. 'That she micht be able to think eneuch o hersel.'

Another form is 'O Lord, gie us a guid conceit o oorsels.'

Ye ken your groats in ither folk's kale.

You recognise your own property even when it is embodied in another person's handiwork.

Walter Scott was reminded of this proverb by an old wife whose tales and sayings he had introduced into his works.

Ye look like a Lochaber axe.

Highly aggressive. The Lochaber axe was a sort of pike with a curved axe on one side and a pick on the other. The Edinburgh Town Guard, usually Highlanders, carried them. Robert Fergusson records that they used them rather freely.

Jock Bell gaed furth to play his freaks
Great cause he had to rue it.
For frae a stark Lochaber axe
He gat a clamihewit
Fu sair that nicht.

'Ye look like a runner,' quo the deil to the lobster.

The lobster is the speediest beast in the sea, even though he swims tail first.

Ye maun either do or die.

Burns used this in the final line of *Scots Wha Hae*.

Ye may as weel try to lift the milkin stane o Dumbarton.

The 'Milking Stone' of Dumbarton is a very large boulder which fell from Dumbarton Castle Rock and traditionally killed a number of women milking cows in the meadow.

The proverb means 'You are attempting the impossible.'

Ye may tak drink oot o a burn when ye canna tak a bite oot o the brae.

Many died of starvation in old Scotland, nobody of thirst.

Ye may hae a guid memory but ye hae puir judgement.
> A rebuke to those who bring up a subject inopportunely.

Ye may think on your cradle
I'll think on my stane
And there'll ne'er be an heir
To Knockdolion again.
> Knockdolion is a conspicuous conical hill, a landmark for
> ships entering the Firth of Clyde. A mermaid used to sit on
> a stone near Knockdolion House and sing all night,
> disturbing the lady of the house, who had the stone broken
> up. The mermaid returned only once, to sing the above
> swan-song. Soon after, the cradle was overturned, the
> infant heir dead, and the family became extinct.

Ye ne'er heard a fisher cry stinking fish.

Ye ne'er see green cheese but your een reel.
> Green cheese means cheese newly-made: a great tempt-
> ation to gourmands.

Ye run for the spurtle when the pot's boiling over.
> The spurtle was a rod for stirring porridge etc. Every
> nation has a proverb on these lines, the English one being
> about locking the stable-door after the horse is stolen.

Ye shape shune by your ain shauchled feet.
> You judge all characters by your own, and it is deformed.

Ye wad dae little for God an the deil was deid.
> A cynical thought expressed also in this way: 'A kirk
> withoot a Hell is no worth a damned dockan.'

Ye wad gar men trow that spade shafts bore honey pears.
> Honey pears were the sweet variety as opposed to the
> harsher kinds grown for medicinal purposes.

Ye wad kiss ony man's dirty shune for leave to bake in his oven.

Ye wad say that aback o the Hirsel Law.
>You seem very outspoken but you would not dare to say that in the hearing of a powerful man such as the Earl of Home, whose seat, the Hirsel, lies to the south of the Hirsel Law, near Coldstream.

Ye wad wheedle a laverock frae the lift.
>You have a winning way with you.

Ye was put oot o the oven for nippin the pies.
>You can't keep your fingers off other people's property.

Ye winna believe a bannock's hardened unless ye knock on it wi your nail.
>Description of a doubting Thomas.

Ye would be a guid piper's bitch; ye smell oot the weddins.
>A scoffing reply to a gossip who envisaged certain matches between couples. The piper's dog, had, of course, an interest in finding business for his master, who attended the weddings to provide music, but the gossip had not even that excuse.

Ye'll be a man afore your mither.
>Little boys were often promised this.

Ye'll gang up the Lawnmarket yet.
>The only road to the gallows in the Grassmarket, from the Old Tolbooth or 'Heart of Midlothian' (which stood on the west side of St. Giles' Cathedral, and is now marked by an ornamental heart of paving stones) was by way of the Lawnmarket and the West Bow. The last execution there was in 1784, after which public executions were held, as anciently, at the Tolbooth until the 1820's, when they were performed within the precincts of the Calton Jail.

Ye'll no sell your hen on a wet day.
>On a wet day a hen has little glamour.

69

Ye'll hae anither Lord Soulis mistake.

Some person complained to King Robert the Bruce about Lord Soulis. Bruce jokingly told them to go and boil him if they liked, little expecting that they would take him at his word.

'Ye're a liar,' said the dummy;
'Sae I see,' said the blin' man;
'Weel, dinna shout sae lood,' said the deaf man.

They were all cheats. In olden times, after bad harvests, great numbers of beggars swarmed over Scotland, and many professed to be physically afflicted. 'Sorning', or begging by force, was heavily punished under the later Jameses. In the 18th century beggars were given licences.

Ye're as learnt as a scholar o Buckhaven College.

Robert Chambers in a Picture of Scotland 1827 says that the folk of Buckhaven, Fife, were unjustly described as peculiarly rude in manners and speech and supposedly descended from the crew of a Brabant vessel wrecked in Fife in the reign of Philip II. In the National Library of Scotland there is a broadside of 1718 representing Buckhaven ironically as a great seminary of learning and a place where the elegancies of life were carried to an unexampled pitch of perfection. This lampooning had earned Buckhaven the title of 'The Gotham of Scotland,' The College (i.e. University) of Buckhaven was in Chamber's day 'a goodly old-fashioned house of two stories with two outside stairs facing the shore, about the centre of the village.'

Ye're buttoned up the back like Achmahoy's dogs.

Your vertebrae are showing.

Ye're come to fetch fire.

You are on a short visit for your own advantage. When a house-fire went out, (this being before the era of matches or even of flint and steel, it seems) a neighbour had to oblige with hot coals, or a glowing peat.

70

Ye're feard for the day ye never saw.
>You are worrying unnecessarily.

Ye're like a hen on a het girdle.
>You can't keep still.

Ye're like the coo-couper o Swinton, your thirst's unquenchable.
>This cattle salesman's explanation of his drouth was that at his birth the midwife had given him an over-long drink of salt water. A two-fold reason for giving new-born infants brine was: it brought up the phlegm and drove out the devil.

You've been eating sourocks instead o lang kail.
>Sourocks or sorrel is said by Culpeper 'to cool fevers and to quench thirst and to promote appetite in a decaying stomach' but here it means 'you are in a sour mood'.

Your breid's baket, ye may hing up your girdle.
>You have achieved all you aimed at.

Your conscience is like a grey friar's sleeve.
>Very accommodating.

Your meat will mak you bonny and when you're bonny you'll be weel lo'ed and when you're weel lo'ed you'll be licht-herted and when you're licht-herted you'll loup far.
>This far-fetched argument was recited to encourage children to eat.

Your mind's aye chasin mice.
>'Your wits are wool-gathering' is the English proverb.

Your tongue gaes like a lamb's tail.
>You are never done talking.

Eneuch's eneuch o breid and cheese.

71

Gaelic Proverbs

In a book of Scots proverbs it would be a great sin of omission not to represent a variety of Gaelic proverbs, which review every field of human activity from the unique standpoint of the Gaelic Celt.

Anail a' Ghàidheil—air a' mhullach.
> The Gael's breathing-place—on the summit.

An rud a ni math do bhàillidh Dhiura cha dean e cron do'n Rùsgan MacPhàil.
> What's good for the Jura factor will do no harm to Fleecy MacPhail.
> On Fleecy going to pay his rent the factor drank from a whisky flask saying: 'I think you are better without this.'
> But Fleecy helped himself to an equally large drink, passing the above remark.

Baobh sam bith a ni guidhe, far an teoth' an goal, 's ann a's truim' am buille.
> When a wicked woman curses, where the love is hottest there the blow is heaviest.

Bogha dh'iughar Easragain
Ite firein Locha-Trèig
Cèir bhuidhe Bhaile-na-Gailbhinn
'S ceann bho'n cheard MacPheidearain.
> Bow from yew of Esragin
> Eagle feather from Loch Treig
> Yellow wax from Galway Town
> Arrow head by MacPhederan.
> Ingredients for the archer, MacPhederan was a famous arrowsmith.

Cha b'e sin an salann saor.
> That was no cheap salt. (i.e. an expensive extra)
> Charles II (1669) introduced a salt tax, and the salt tax imposed after the Union of 1707 killed the Scottish continental salt fish trade. As late as 1800 salt was taxed to forty times its cost. Of course, as Gandhi showed in India, there was plenty free salt in the ocean.

Cha chumadh an Righ snaoisean ris a gaoth.
> The King himself couldn't keep the wind in snuff.

Cha'thainig ian glan riamh a' nead a' chlamhain.
> Clean bird never came out of a kite's nest.
> Some birds keep their nests scrupulously clean but kites' nests were notoriously foul. Kites are now very rare, even in the Highlands.

Cha'n ann de mo chuideachd thu, ars an colman.
> You are not of my flock, said the dove.
> Imitative of the cooing of the cushat-doo, or woodpigeon.

Cha'n 'eil earbsa sa bith ri'chur anns na h-Eileanaich.
> There's no trust to be put in the Islanders (the weather was so uncertain, for one thing.)

Cha'n fhiach ordugh oidhche.
> Night orders are not good (being hard to carry out).

Chi mi sin, 's fuaighidh mi seo.
> 'That I see but this I sew.'
> That was the non-committal reply to the ghost, of the little tailor of Beauly, who undertook to stitch up a suit at night in the haunted ruin of Kilchrist Church. He barely escaped from the grisly spectre that rose from a tomb to murder him.

73

Clanna nan Gaidheal 'an guailibh a chéile.
>The clans of the Gael, shoulder to shoulder.
>History would have turned out far otherwise if they had done this, but they were notoriously given to long feuds. Even in the '45 those who did not rise far outnumbered those who did.

Clann Diarmid nam busa dubha cuiribh riu 'us beireabh orra.
>The MacDiarmids of the black mouths, go at them and catch them.
>Probably a war-cry of the Macdonalds or the Macgregors, used perhaps at Inverlochy where the Campbells were defeated by Montrose in 1645.

Cuiridh peirceall na caorn'n crann air an fharadh.
>The sheep's jaw will put the plough on the hen-roost.
>A dark saying of the Brahan seer about the turning of the crofting lands into great sheep runs.

Deoch-an-doruis.
>The stirrup-cup, or one for the road, in the good old days when the vehicle was directed and drawn by a strictly teetotal quadruped.

Facal ann, a Mhaighstir Iain, 's am Brugh a lionadh.
>Get on with it, Mr. John, the channel is filling.
>Rev. John McLean, Kilninian, Mull, preaching on the tidal island of Gometra, took rather long over his final prayer so this was the stage whisper from his beadle that rang through the small church.

Fear eil' air son Eachainn.
>Another man for Hector.
>The MacLeans suffered a great slaughter at Inverkeithing (1652) in the Civil War, but came forward despite this, each man crying the above as he fell on the foe.

Gabh eòlas Rudh-a-bhàird air.
> Take it like the Bard's Point (i.e. keep away!).
> The Bard's Point was a dangerous promontory, so wise
> sailors avoided it completely.

Is cruaidh an t'Earrach anns an cùnnt na faoghagan.
> It's a hard spring when the whelks are counted.
> Whelks were the main food of the islanders and shores-
> folk, when the potatoes, salt-fish and meal were ex-
> hausted.

Is fhada Dunéideann bho'n fhear 'tha' eirigh's a' Stoir.
> Edinburgh is far from the man who rises at Stoer.
> Like the saying: 'It's a far cry to Lochow.'
> The authority of Edinburgh did not run as far as Stoer in
> West Sutherland.

Is ioma muthadh a thig air an oidhche fhada Gheamhraidh.
> Many a change comes in the long winter night.
> That was the enigmatic hint made by one of the company
> of Campbell soldiers to his MacIan host before the
> Glencoe Massacre, enabling him and his family to escape.
> But most of the MacIans got no warning.

*Leathaineach gun bhòsd; Dònullach gun tapadh; Caimbeulach
gun mhórchuis.*
> A MacLean without boast; a MacDonald without clever-
> ness; a Campbell without pride.
> Three rarities, according to this judge of character, who
> lumped each clan together as if they were species of
> animals.

Ludh an spioraidh, 'dol timchioll na drochaid.
> The way of the ghost, going round the bridge.
> *Domhnull Mòr a' bhochdain,* or Big Donald of the ghost,
> was troubled with a kind of perpetual second sight and
> could not shake off his annoying acquaintance. He was
> advised to emigrate to Philadelphia, but the first person he

met on the quayside was the ghost. Donald thought there was enough running water in the Atlantic to stop the ghost following him, but apparently did not know that, the Bering Strait being frozen, there was a land route round by Siberia. This conversation took place:

"Camar a thainig thus' an seo? (How came you here?)"
"Thainig mi mu'n cuairt. (I came round about.)"

Millidh smugaid cuideachd.
   A spittal will spoil a company.
   The Highlanders were not much addicted to this good old Yankee indoor sport.

GLOSSARY

Scots	*English*	*Scots*	*English*

abune—above.

ae—one; single.

agley—wrong; off the line.

aik—oak.

ain—own.

airn—iron.

ane—one.

bairns—children.

banning—cursing.

bannock—unleavened cake.

bawbee—halfpenny.

beckit—curtseyed.

beetle—mallet.

bield—shelter.

bigget—built

birk—birch-tree.

birse—shoemaker's bristle.

black-dockit—with a black behind.

blate—shy.

bodle—small coin.

bogles—bogey-men.

bouk—bulk; size.

brae—hill.

branned—served by the boar.

breed o—related to.

breeks—breeches.

broo or bree—broth; gravy.

brugh—ring of mist.

bubbly-jock—turkey-cock.

bumbee—bumble-bee.

bummer—hummer.

buskit—dressed up; prepared for show.

ca—drive.

ca'—call.

caller—fresh.

canny—careful.

carl hemp—strong hemp fibre.

carle's win—man's crop; harvest.

chack—large hunk.

chafts—jaws.

chiel—fellow.

clap—hare's form.

clok—beetle.

cog—wooden bowl.

coo—cow.

coo-couper—cow salesman.

coul—cap.

corbie—raven.

cour—cower.

croon o the causey—highest point of roadway.

crouse—happy.

crowdie—kind of brose.

daft—giddy; foolish.

daur—dare.

daw—untidy woman.

daws—dawns.

deen—done (Buchan).

deils—devils.

delved—dug.

ding—push; strike.

dozens—settles; fades away.

draff—pig-feed.

dreich—dry; dull.

dub—puddle.

dule—sorrow.

dummy—dumb person.

dunts—blows.

ee; een—eye; eyes.

Embro—Edinburgh.

emot—ant.

faur—where (Buchan).

fain—anxious.

farrest—farthest.

fashed—bothered.

feard—afraid.

fettle—condition; health.

file—dirty.

fizzes—froths.

flesh-flees—blue-bottles.

flichter—fluttering.

flittin—removing.

fremit—strange.

fuff—noise made by blowing
out breath.

gab—talk; mouth.

gae—go; gave.

gaislin—gosling.

gang—go.

gansel—honk; harsh sauce.

gaun—going.

gar—to force.

gear—possessions.

geary—wealthy.

gerss—grass.

giff-gaff—exchange of goods.

girdle—flat iron plate for baking.

girning—complaining.

Gramacie—magic spell.

grace—mercy.

grat—wept.

greet—weep.

grice—young pig.

groats—crushed oats.

grosset; grossart—gooseberry.

grumph—grunt.

guid; gude—good.

gudeman—husband.

gudewife—wife.

gustin-bane—stock-bone.

gule—corn marigold.

hag-pen—bog-hole.

hanselled—brought a lucky gift.

harns—brains.

haud doon—to bully.

hauf—half.

hause—throat.

herries—robs.

het—hot; uncomfortable.

houtie-croutie—buttocks.

howdie—midwife.

hure—harlot.

ilka—each.

ill—bad.

ingleside—fireside.

Janaveer—January.

78

jaw—rough shower.

John Heezlum-Peezlum—Man in the Moon.

jouk—dodge.

kail—broth; kind of cabbage.

kail-blade—cabbage-leaf.

kebbuck—cheese.

kenna—know not.

kep—herd; protect; keep; catch.

kirk—church.

kirn—churn; fireside concert.

kitchen—relish.

Laigh (the)—Lowlands.

lang kail—unchopped cabbage.

lang syne—long ago.

lave—remainder.

laverock—skylark.

lear—learning.

leglingirth—lowest hoop of milk pail.

lichtlied—spoke contemptuously.

lichtsome—pleasant.

lift—sky.

linn—a gorge through which a torrent flows.

lintie—linnet.

loaning—country lane.

loose—louse.

lowp—jump.

lug—ear.

maik—equal.

maun—must.

meal-kist—meal-chest.

meikle; muckle; mickle—great.

mennans—minnows.

mim—demure; shy.

minny—pet name for mother.

mirk—dark.

mowdies—moles.

muffed—gloved; mittened.

nay-say—refusal.

neb—nose.

new-come—newly begun.

nicker—neigh.

nocht—nothing.

oo or woo—wool.

or—before; ere.

parritch—porridge.

Pasch—Easter.

peesweep—green plover.

piece—slice of bread.

pike—pick.

preein—tasting; trying.

pykin—plucking.

quo—said; quoth.

raip—rope.

ramskin—parchment.

rattans—rats.

raws—rows of cottages.

reuch—rough.

riggin—roof-top.

riving—tearing.

rumple-routie—nonsense word perhaps meaning crossed fingers.

sab—sob.

saipet—soaped.

sairer—sorer.

sandy-mills—sand-castles.

sark—chemise; shirt.

saugh—willow.

saut—salt.

scarting—scratching.

Schew!—Get off with you!

schools—shovels.

schored—warned.

schule—school.

sea-maws—seagulls.

shauchled—shapeless; broken-down.

shoon—shoes.

sic—such.

siller—money; silver.

simmer—summer.

skailed—emptied.

soo—sow.

sooms—swims.

sourocks—common sorrel.

soutar—shoemaker.

speer—ask.

Spunky—Will-o'-Wisp.

spurtle—porridge-stick.

stang—sting.

stark-deid—stone-dead.

steekit—shut.

stey—steep.

stirkie—bullock.

stoor—dust.

straucht—straight.

sturts—startles.

tae—one.

tane and the tither—one and the other.

teuch—tough.

thack—thatch.

thole—bear; endure.

tint—lost.

tip—take the ram.

tocherless—without dowry.

tod—fox.

toom—empty.

tout (pun)—sound of a horn or female pudendum.

trow—believe.

vreet (Buchan)—writing.

wae—sad; sorrow.

wame—belly; stomach.

wark—fuss; trouble.

waught—long drink.

waukrife—unable to sleep.

waur—worse.

whangs—slices.

whin—gorse; furze.

widdie—gallows.

wispit—wiped with hay.

woo or oo—wool.

wrocht—brought about; worked.

wyce—wise, sensible.

yerk—jerk; stitch sharply.

yett—gate.